Religions of the World

Sylvia Bates

Macdonald Educational

26

28

set up

34 **Islam**
The life of Mohammed. How he
became a prophet of Allah.

46 Index

Contents

How to use
This book d
as some of
at the cont
listed. For
you will f
The inde
subject i
of it. A
page 25

Pa

▲ An American Indian totem pole from the north west coast. A number of animals could be featured on one pole. Some tribes thought they were related to these animals and considered them sacred.

A Celtic tribe may well have been frightened by an eclipse of the sun. ▶

6

Early man

No one knows how religions began. One suggestion is that they were early man's answers to big questions which puzzled them. They wondered about the things and events they saw around them. They looked for explanations for the rising and setting of the sun and moon. They were frightened by thunder and lightning. They wanted to know what happened to men when they died. They believed invisible gods or spirits were the powers which made these things happen.

Organized religions

Most early men lived and travelled together in very small groups. Even though they had to struggle to survive, their lives were fairly simple. However as tribal societies developed and people started living together in greater numbers, their lives became more complex. It became necessary to make rules so that they could live peacefully together. Many of these rules concerned man's relationship with the gods and most men tried not to break them, because they did not want to make the gods angry.

Holy places

Special places were established where men talked to the gods and where they offered them gifts. Some wise men became servants of the gods, and looked after the holy places. They taught people how to please the gods. People also began to believe that there was another life after death and they looked for ways to achieve this.

The development of religions

During the past few thousand years, wise men in India, China and the countries of the Middle East have taught men the value of belief in a God or gods. They showed how this kind of spiritual faith and the effort to lead a good life could result in life after death. Millions of people continue to follow these teachings. Religion has helped to civilize and educate. It has made some men kinder, more gentle, more understanding and more willing to help each other.

Ancient Egypt

Egypt was one of the earliest civilizations. The Egyptians built cities along the River Nile. They had laws and they developed a form of writing, made up of tiny pictures called *hieroglyphics*. Like other nations, they believed that natural happenings such as the annual flooding of the Nile were controlled by gods. The ruler of the Egyptians was called the Pharaoh, whom they believed to be a god.

The gods

Some Egyptian gods were like animals, others like humans, and some a mixture of animal and human form, like Anubis The guide of human souls. By 2,500 BC Ra, the sun god, was recognized as the most important god. However the Egyptians continued to fear other gods and goddesses. Osiris, god of the Nile was particularly respected. This was because they could only grow crops on the land beside the Nile for the rest of the country was desert.

Priests

The gods were served by priests, highly educated men who lived in the temples of the gods and who were easily recognizable by their shaven heads and glistening white robes. In addition to looking after the temples, priests taught mathematics, medicine and literature. They wrote on sheets made from the water plant, papyrus, which they joined together to make long scrolls. They provide a clear account of Egypt's religion.

◄ A Sumerian work of art. The tree may represent the 'Tree of life'. The Sumerians were a very early civilization. They settled in an area bounded by the two rivers Tigris and Euphrates. We have been able to learn something about their way of life and their religion. They had many gods. Dumuzi was the god of vegetation whom they believed died in winter and was reborn in spring.

They also believed in a life after death, but their picture of the next world was very grim. They thought that the dead sat in darkness dressed in feathers eating dust and clay.

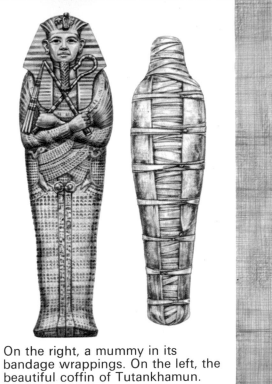

On the right, a mummy in its bandage wrappings. On the left, the beautiful coffin of Tutankhamun.

▲ Anubis, the jackal-headed god, weighs the heart of a dead man against a feather, which stands for truth. Only the good entered the next world.

After life

Egyptians believed that men would live again after death. The Pharaoh and sometimes wealthy citizens arranged for their bodies to be preserved after death and buried in elaborate tombs, together with weapons, food, jewellery and furniture—everything they would need in a future life. These preserved bodies are called *mummies*.

Ceremonies

Because the Egyptians had many gods and each god had its own temple, there were a great many temples in ancient Egypt. Ordinary people were not allowed in the temples, only the Pharaoh, the priests and a few important people. Each day, the priest burned incense, a kind of perfume, as an offering, opened the doors of the shrine, and removed the god. The image was undressed, then washed and reclothed for the new day. After a feast had been offered to the god, the image was put back in the shrine, and the doors were sealed until the following day.

Festivals

At festival times the gods were taken from their temples and paraded through the streets.

The two things that interested most Egyptians were children and crops. The formal festivals were supervised by the priests. The gods were asked to provide mothers with healthy children and the country with a good harvest.

The religion of ancient Egypt lasted well into the time of the Roman Empire.

Greece and Rome

The gods and goddesses of the highly civilized people of ancient Greece lived on Mount Olympus in northern Greece and although they were very powerful, they were not perfect. They had human form and could be jealous and cruel, fall in love or make war just like human beings, but on a larger scale.

Zeus was the mightiest of the gods, he saw everything that happened and had unlimited power. The remaining gods each took an interest in a particular part of human affairs; for example Athene was goddess of war. The Greeks built temples for their gods, where they sacrificed animals, praying for the gods' help in producing healthy children or a good harvest.

The Olympic Games

The original games began 2,800 years ago and were held at Olympia, in honour of Zeus. They combined religious ceremonies with competition in the arts and athletics.

The Emperor Augustus. He was Julius Caesar's nephew and successor. People believed he was a god.

Hades was the Greek god of the dead. To reach his kingdom, souls of the dead had to cross the River Styx. They were rowed across by Charon. On the far bank stood Cerberus, the three-headed dog.

Rome

The Romans adopted many of the Greek religious beliefs. Like the Greeks they worshipped a family of gods, giving each Greek god a Roman name; for example Zeus became Jupiter, and Poseidon, the Greek sea god, became Neptune.

Emperor worship

The Emperor Augustus, who succeeded Julius Caesar, inherited a country ruined by civil war. During his reign Rome became peaceful and prosperous and people began to believe that Augustus himself was superhuman. The idea of the Emperor as a god, and that the soldiers and citizens from all the countries under Roman rule paid their respects to him by sprinkling incense in an altar fire, became one means of uniting the Roman Empire. Emperor worship became part of the official religion. Temples were built in Rome and throughout the Empire and dedicated to the emperor of the time.

°Salt Lake City

North America

*The red star indicates
those areas under
Communist
governments.*

Canterbury

Geneva
Lourdes °

Judaism
Followers: 13,000,000

Christianity
Followers: 1,220 million

Islam
Followers: 580 million

Hinduism
Followers: 480 million

Buddhism
Followers: 300 million

China
Followers: 410 million.
This figure combines
all different faiths.

Japan
Followers: 163 million.
Shinto and Buddhism.

 Tribal

 Uninhabited

South America

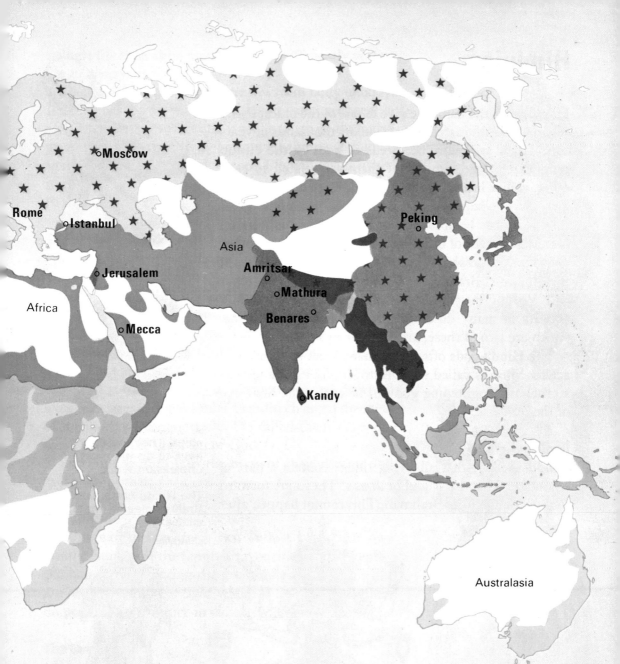

Moscow

Rome

Istanbul

Jerusalem

Africa

Mecca

Asia

Amritsar

Mathura

Benares

Kandy

Peking

Australasia

Religion today

There are perhaps three main reasons why a religion
might spread from one country to another: conquest,
war, and persecution; missionaries setting out to con-
vert people of a different faith; and finally the emigra-
tion of people seeking a better life in a new country.

Hindu life

Some Hindus hope to be united with Brahman through Yoga. This is a form of meditation where the person sits in a special position, breathes in a special way and clears his mind of all thought. He tries to control his mind and body by strict self discipline.

Weddings

Weddings take place in any appropriate room or hall. Guests are invited and bring presents. The bride and groom exchange garlands of flowers, which they place round their necks. The bride is given to the groom by her father. For the first time, she will have the red spot in the centre of her forehead, which all married Hindu women wear. The priest speaks to the couple about the meaning of marriage. The holy fire is lit in a special metal bowl. This represents God, and the couple take seven steps around it, making promises to each other about the future. Weddings are happy affairs and are followed by a feast.

Divali

During the festival of Divali, lights of all sorts are lit in temples, houses and streets. Decorations are put up, fireworks are let off and processions in honour of the gods pass through the streets. At home, people have parties and pray to Lakshmi, goddess of wealth, thanking her for the past year and asking her blessing for the year ahead.

Divali is also regarded as a new beginning. It is the start of a new business year. People clean their homes and put on new clothes. It is a time of great happiness for Hindus everywhere.

Holi

The festival of *Holi* celebrates the coming of spring and honours the god Krishna. People wear bright clothes and spray each other with coloured water and powder. Images of demons are burnt in the streets. Holi is a high-spirited and colourful festival.

A wandering Sadhu. They devote their lives and thoughts to the gods. They beg their food from other Hindus.

▲ The Holy city of Benares through which flows the sacred River Ganges. A Hindu will try to bathe in the river. He believes this will free him from his sins. After his death, his body will be burned and his ashes scattered on the river.

A bride and groom are seated on the floor during a Hindu wedding. They wear garlands of flowers.

Buddhism

The word Buddha means 'the Enlightened One'. It is a title given to Prince Siddhartha Gautama, who lived in India about 2,500 years ago.

The life of Buddha

He was a Hindu and for many years he lived a happy life with his family. This ended when he became aware of sickness, old age and death. He wondered how men could escape from endless suffering, dying and rebirth.

▲ The wheel is an important symbol to both Hindus and Buddhists. It can suggest the cycle of birth, death and reincarnation. The eight spokes can also represent the Buddhist eight-fold path.

At the age of 29, he left his home and family, cut off his hair, put on a yellow robe and lived the life of a penniless holy man. For many years he tried to find the answer to his problem. At last, sitting under a special tree called the Bo Tree

A children's ceremony showing the three stages in the Buddha's life.▼

The boy is dressed in rich robes, for Buddha was once a prince.

His head is shaved and he wears rags so that he looks like a holy man.

He wears monk's robes and spends time in a monastery.

▲ The Buddha sits meditating in the shade of the Bo Tree.

he was enlightened, he believed he had found the answer.

He saw that happiness came through men controlling their desires, not through worshipping gods. He produced the Four Noble Truths and the Eightfold Path to enlightenment.

The Four Noble Truths

1 Suffering is part of life.
2 Suffering is due to selfishness.
3 Suffering will stop if selfishness is crushed.
4 The way to crush selfishness is to follow the Eightfold Path.

The Eightfold Path

1 Accept the Four Noble Truths.
2 Think in the right way which leads you to help others.
3 Be kind in speech, avoid boasting, gossip and lies.
4 Do what is right.
5 Earn your living in a way which is good.
6 Avoid evil thoughts and actions and work hard.
7 Learn to concentrate.
8 Be at peace in your mind.

He taught men that if they followed this way of life, they would lose their desire for things which brought unhappiness. They would reach Nirvana, a state of happiness which would release them from the round of death and rebirth.

Monks

The *Sangha* is the Buddhist order of monks and nuns. Originally this was made up of wandering beggars who lived in caves or houses only in the rainy season. Their main occupation was to teach the Buddha's message.

China and Japan

Buddhism reached China and Japan from India. It became popular in both countries, without destroying the ancient religions already in existence. Chinese and Japanese Buddhists follow the Mahayana or Northern Way. They believe that Buddha himself is a god who can help men to follow the Eightfold Path.

Taoism and Confucianism in China

Tao means the Way, in which men live a life of moderation, avoiding extremes of any kind. The secret of happiness is to live naturally without trying to be different or change things.

Kung Fu-tse, the founder of Confucianism, believed that happiness could best be achieved by having rules for everyday life. He taught that kindness, respect and loyalty were important and if everyone tried to live according to these ideas, men would live in peace.

Shinto

The ancient religion of Japan is Shinto, meaning the Way of the Gods. The Japanese worshipped and still worship many hundreds of gods or spirits of nature.

Shinto is still an important part of Japanese life and the Japanese believe that the spirits can influence events and affect their daily lives.

Shrines

The dwelling places of the gods are regarded as holy places or shrines. Buildings are erected to contain something sacred to the god, a stone, a sword, a

Chinese women praying at the Babies Altar in a Taoist temple in Peking.

piece of cloth or lock of hair. A shrine can be recognized by its Tori or gateway. The Tori symbolizes the passage from everyday life into the holy presence of a god.

Worship

A Japanese prays to his favourite spirit by visiting the shrine to thank him and to make an offering of rice or money. Priests look after the shrines. Small babies are taken there to obtain the gods' blessing and throughout their lives, the Japanese visit shrines on important occasions like marriage, getting a job, gaining promotion or upon retirement.

At home

Most Japanese homes contain a *Kami-danu* or godshelf. On this there is a tablet containing the names of the family's favourite gods and a small lamp. The first rice cooked each day is put on the shelf with rice wine and rice cakes, to honour the gods.

▲ Young Japanese schoolgirls in Buddhist contemplation, or deep thought.

The floating Tori at Itsukushima Shinto Shrine, Japan. The Tori represents the passage from everyday life into the presence of the spirits.▼

Sikhs, Jains, Parsees

All these religions are based in India. The Sikh religion is in some ways a combination of some Hindu beliefs and some of Islam. It was founded by Nanak, a guru or teacher. Sikhs believe in one God, called Nam, meaning 'the Name'. They worship their God in temples which contain no images, only their holy books, the *Adi Granth*. Services in the temples consist of prayers, reading the sacred book, and making offerings. Worshippers often share a meal after the service.

The five K's

Sikh men honour the five K's, which are symbols of their faith.

1 Kesha—Hair on the head and face is left uncut. The head is usually covered by a turban.
2 Kangha—The comb which fastens the hair beneath the turban.
3 Kachha—shorts.
4 Kara—A steel bracelet, worn on the right wrist.
5 Kirpan—A sword, for self defence.

Warriors

Sikhs are known as brave fighting men, probably because they have often had to fight for their existence. They all have the name 'Singh' meaning lion, in addition to their family names.

Jains

Jains believe that everything in nature has a soul. Jains will never take life and will always try to avoid injuring any living thing. They are vegetarians which means they do not eat meat. The strictest

▲ The Golden Temple at Amritsar which is the Sikhs' most famous city.
Jains wearing cloth masks to avoid swallowing insects by accident. ▼

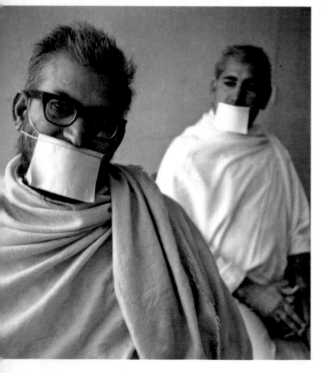

Jains will sweep away insects from their path to avoid treading on them, and wear a cloth mask to prevent the accidental swallowing of an insect.

Like Hindus, they believe in reincarnation and that good deeds decide whether a man will be reborn in a higher or lower state.

Their temples contain images of the 24 conquerors. Worshippers pray to these images and make them offerings, usually of rice. They use the swastika, an ancient Indian sign, as a symbol of well being.

Parsees

Twenty-six centuries ago, Zoroastra taught the people of Persia to destroy their old gods and to believe in one true God called Ahura Mazda, or Lord Wisdom. An evil god was constantly at war with Ahura Mazda and men were urged to lead good lives and thus help God in his fight against evil.

A good life would be rewarded by life after death and this could be accomplished by good thoughts, good works, and good deeds.

Parsees worship in temples where a sacred fire is always kept burning. There are no statues or images. Worshippers bring gifts which the priests burn in the sacred fire. Members of other religions are forbidden to enter Parsee temples.

Towers of Silence

Parsees are not allowed to burn or bury their dead. Instead they place the bodies of the dead on 'Towers of Silence' where vultures eat the flesh. When the bones fall into the pit below, they are destroyed by lime.

▲ A Sikh wearing the traditional turban.
A Parsee temple in Bombay, India. Members of other religions are not allowed to enter. ▼

Judaism

Judaism is the religion of the Jews or Hebrews who, hundreds of years ago, lived in Palestine, now called Israel. Their religion is based on their history and their special relationship with God.

One God

Jews believe that 4,000 years ago, God made a covenant or agreement with their ancestor, Abraham. Abraham lived in the city of Ur, in Sumeria, and, unlike the people around him, believed there was only one true God. Guided by God, he left Ur and settled with his family in Palestine. The descendants of Abraham continued to believe that God considered them to be his chosen people.

The Exodus

Several hundred years after Abraham's death, the Jews had moved into Egypt where they later worked as slaves. Instructed by God, their leader Moses took them out of Egypt into the desert between Egypt and Palestine.

▲ The blowing of the Shofar, or ram's horn.

God tests Abraham by commanding him to sacrifice his son, Isaac. God relents and the ram is killed instead. ▼

They stayed there for forty years. During this time Moses received from God the Ten Commandments and other laws which the Jews were told to keep.

The Promised Land

Finally the Jews reached Palestine, their Promised Land, and conquering the people who lived there, they settled down to follow God's laws.

Their holy books, in the form of scrolls, containing God's laws are called the *Torah* and the *Talmud*. The Talmud explains how these laws should be obeyed in daily living. Jewish places of worship are called synagogues and their leaders are Rabbis. Some Jews believe that God will one day send a Messiah or Saviour, who will bring peace and happiness to the world.

A turbulent history

Since their escape from Egypt, the Jews have suffered invasion by other nations, and exile in other lands. When they rebelled against the Romans during the first century AD they were turned out of their land and scattered throughout the Middle East and Europe. They remained faithful to their beliefs and followed God's laws.

▲ A Jewish scroll.

David saves the Israelites by killing Goliath, the champion of the Philistines. David was a shepherd boy who later became king. ▼

Jewish customs

Shabbat or Sabbath is the Jewish day of rest, beginning at sunset on Friday and ending at sunset on Saturday. It is a family occasion and at the evening meal, the table is lit by candlelight. The men wear their cappels (skull caps). The father of the family says a prayer and blesses the wine and the bread. Jewish families are strengthened and brought closer together by sharing this religious feast each week.

Kosher
The Jews have very strict laws about the food they eat. They do not eat pork or shellfish and must buy their meat from Kosher butchers, who slaughter animals in a special way so that the meat is drained of blood. Rabbis have to make sure that the animals are killed correctly. Meat and milk have to be kept apart. After a meal in which meat has been eaten, three hours must pass before any milk can be drunk.

The synagogue
Services in the synagogue consist of prayer, a talk by the Rabbi and a reading of the Torah, which is taken from the Ark, or box, where it is always kept. The Torah is in the form of a large scroll and it is carried in procession to a special reading desk.

Bar Mitzvah
The proudest moment of a Jewish boy's life is the ceremony of *Bar Mitzvah*. This happens soon after a boy's thirteenth birthday. He reads aloud from the Torah during a special service and after this, he is a full member of his community.

◀A Bar Mitzvah ceremony is being held out of doors in Jerusalem.
   Jerusalem is the holy city of the Jews. It was conquered by King David, who made it his capital. His son, Solomon, built a great temple there.

Hassidic Jews are shown praying at the Wailing Wall in Jerusalem. They are a very strict sect.
   The Wailing Wall is the only part of the Sacred Temple still standing. The rest of the Temple was destroyed in AD 70 by the Romans. ▶

Passover

Passover is one of the Jews' chief religious festivals. It is in memory of the escape of the Jews from Egypt. At the feast, the story of their leaving Egypt is told and everything they eat has a special meaning. The unleavened or flat bread reminds them of the flight, when there was no time for the bread to be left to rise.

Yom Kippur

Yom Kippur, the Day of Atonement is the most holy day of all. Jews fast, (go without food) and pray for forgiveness for their sins. At the end of the day, the *Shofar*, a huge ram's horn trumpet, is blown. It is a time for the remembrance of the dead, and a time to forget quarrels; a time when people feel close to God.

The first Christians

Christianity grew out of Judaism, for its founder, Jesus Christ, was a Jew. He was born in Bethlehem in Judea, which was part of the Roman Empire.

At about the age of thirty, Jesus began to travel around Judea, telling people God was about to make his presence felt in a new way. They should be ready for this by accepting each other with love and forgiveness. Jesus healed sick people and worked miracles.

Jesus spent most of his time with poor, unimportant people, and told them that all men were equal in the sight of God. Some Jewish priests feared he would destroy their authority and wanted to get rid of him.

Jesus was arrested and crucified by Roman soldiers. Three days after his death, he was seen by some of his disciples, or followers, apparently alive again. He told

Jesus had to carry his cross to Calvary, where he was then crucified by Roman soldiers. It was men of his own faith who condemned him to death.

them that his death and resurrection were part of God's plan. They should now spread the message of God's love for mankind and the hope of life after death.

The disciples carried the story of Jesus and his return from death all over the Middle East. Believers in Jesus were called Christians.

When Christianity became the official religion of the Roman Empire, Rome became the centre of Christian belief, which was then called Roman Catholicism. The head of the Church was called the Pope and he was regarded as Christ's representative on earth.

When the Roman Empire split into two parts, Rome continued to be the centre of the Roman Catholic Church. In 1054, in the eastern part of the Empire, Christians rejected the authority of the Pope in Rome. Later, in the 16th century, the Church in the west divided again into Protestant and Roman Catholic.

Christianity today

Christians believe that Jesus was the 'Messiah', the son of God who brought God's message of love to mankind. The story of his life is in the New Testament, which forms part of their holy book, the Bible. Sunday is their day of rest and Christians attend church where they worship God through prayer and song.

Holy Communion

The most important service is Holy Communion or Mass. This celebrates the death of Jesus. He suggested it at the last Passover meal before his arrest and execution.

He blessed bread and wine and told his disciples to eat and drink them in memory of him. In Christian churches, the priest blesses the bread and wine and the worshippers receive a piece of bread and sometimes a sip of wine.

Christening or Baptism

Babies are taken to church to be chrisened or named by the priest, with the blessing of the church. He baptises them with holy water and accepts them as members of the Christian community. Close friends or relatives, called godparents, promise to see that the child grows up a good Christian.

Confirmation

Christian boys and girls, when they reach their early teens or even earlier in Catholic countries where they may be seven or eight years old, attend a special service in church, where they show that they understand the teachings of Christ.

▲ The Crucifixion is re-enacted by Mexicans at a religious festival.

A service being held in the beautiful Alexander Nevsky Church in Bulgaria (Orthodox). ▼

They are then accepted as members of the Church.

Weddings

Christian men and women are married in church in a special ceremony where they promise to love and respect each other. The priest gives them God's blessing.

Funerals

Christians hope that when they die they will join God in Heaven and enjoy eternal happiness. A special service is held in church, thanking God for the person who has died and asking God to receive his soul.

Festivals

Christian festivals celebrate important events in the life of Christ. Christmas is regarded as Christ's birthday. Special services are held in church, Christmas carols which tell of Christ's birth are sung and people exchange presents in memory of God's gift of Jesus.

Good Friday is the anniversary of Christ's death by crucifixion. The fact of his death is celebrated by a solemn service in church.

Easter is a joyful time, as it celebrates Christ's return from death.

Carrying out Christ's Teachings

Christians have taken their beliefs to every country in the world. Today it has a larger number of believers than any other organized religion. It has been responsible for the introduction of education, medicine and care for the under privileged in many countries.

A festival which takes place on the coast of Santos in Brazil includes a baptism in the sea.

After the Reformation

During the sixteenth century, a German monk named Luther began to criticize some of the ideas and practices of the Roman Catholic Church. His followers, known as Protestors or Protestants, left the Catholic Church and set up their own independent Protestant Churches.

Nonconformists

During the past four centuries, English Protestants have split into a number of different Churches. However there is now an *ecumenical movement*. This means a coming together of some of the different Churches which share many of the same beliefs.

Presbyterians

These follow the teachings of John Calvin, who believed that God wanted to be worshipped in a very simple fashion, without music or singing. They are now called the United Reformed Church having combined with the Congregationalists.

Pilgrim Fathers

Some very strict Presbyterians became known as Puritans. When they found life difficult in England, they crossed the Atlantic and settled in America.

Quakers

Quakers meet in simple meeting houses instead of churches. They also have no formal sessions, but sit in silence until they feel that God has spoken to them. Quakers refuse to take life and are respected for their honesty.

▲ William Penn was the first Quaker. They are a very gentle sect.

Many of the Puritans fled to America but sometimes they were arrested before they could escape. ▼

Like the Puritans, some Quakers emigrated to America where they founded the state of Pennsylvania, named after their leader, William Penn.

Baptists

Baptists believe that very young children should not be baptised, because they cannot understand the ceremony. They are therefore baptised when they are old enough to think seriously about what they were doing.

Methodism

The largest nonconformists' Church is the Society of Methodists, founded by John Wesley in the eighteenth century. It is less formal than the Church of England and it began by Wesley and his followers taking Christ's message to working people, instead of expecting them to come to church. Methodists spoke at open air services in the cities and in the countryside.

▲ John Wesley founded Methodism. He preached to working people up and down the country.

A baptism in Africa. The pool represents the River Jordan where Christ was baptised. ▼

Islam

Followers of Islam are called Muslims. The first Muslims were Arabs who accepted the prophet Mohammed.

Mohammed was born in Mecca, Arabia, in AD 570. At that time, the Arabs worshipped many idols which were kept in the Ka'aba, a temple in Mecca.

The vision of Mohammed

Mohammed, a merchant and camel driver, knew of the beliefs of Judaism and Christianity in one God. In a vision, he believed he saw the angel Gabriel, who told him there was only one God, Allah, and that Mohammed would be his prophet.

Mohammed began spreading this message to the people of Mecca and as a result, he became very unpopular with the priests of the Ka'aba. His life was in danger if he remained in Mecca, so he fled to the city of Medina. This flight is known as the *Hijra* and Muslims count their years from it.

Mohammed gained many followers in Medina and was finally strong enough to take Mecca, destroy the idols and declare the Ka'ba as a holy place for the religion of Islam, which means obedience to the will of God. Mecca is still the Muslims' most holy city.

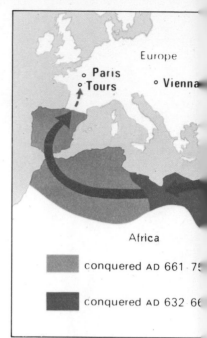

Europe

o Paris
o Tours   o Vienna

Africa

conquered AD 661-75

conquered AD 632-66

▲ The map shows the two main stages in the Muslim expansion. The Muslims were welcomed by many peoples, particularly those who had suffered from the cruelty of some *Byzantine* Christians.

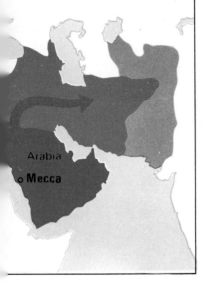

Almost a thousand years later the Turkish Muslims invaded Europe. They were turned back at the siege of Vienna in 1683.

Arabia

o Mecca

An Islamic army marches into the desert. Their conquests took them right into Europe but they were defeated by the Franks in AD 732 at Tours. They remained in Spain till the 15th century.▼

The Qur'an

Muslims believe their faith is not new but a reformed version of the revelation first declared to Adam in the Garden of Eden. The holy book of Islam is the *Qur'an*. It contains the message which God told Mohammed to preach. Five basic rules called the Five Pillars of Wisdom are important to all Muslims. These are:

1 Believe in Allah as the only God.
2 Praying five times each day.
3 Helping the poor.
4 Keeping the Feast of Ramadan.
5 Making a pilgrimage to Mecca.

Muslims believe in life after death, though only those who follow Mohammed's teachings will reach Heaven. Much of Mohammed's teaching is similar to the beliefs of Judaism and Christianity. Abraham and other great men of Jewish history are regarded as prophets, as is Jesus Christ, though Muslims do not regard him as the son of God.

The spread of Islam

Mohammed encouraged Muslims to spread the beliefs of Islam, by war if necessary. In a comparatively short time after Mohammed's death, his religion spread throughout Arabia, across North Africa and throughout the Middle East to India.

▲ Pilgrims praying at the Ka 'aba. The holy Black Stone possibly came from a meteorite.

A lamb is sacrificed at Ramadan, a festival which celebrates the first time Gabriel spoke to Mohammed. ▼

Islamic life

Muslims take their religion very seriously and try to follow the teachings of the Qur'an. Five times a day, they are called to prayer. They wash their face, hands and feet and pray facing Mecca.

Muslim children recite from the Qur'an each day and learn Allah's teachings on marriage, divorce, the duties of parents and employers.

Ramadan

During the month of *Ramadan*, Muslims over ten years old go without food and drink during the hours of daylight. It celebrates the first time God's angel, Gabriel, spoke to Mohammed. Ramadan ends with the festival of *Id-Al-Fitr*, when Muslims celebrate with a party for friends and relatives.

Pilgrimage

Every Muslim is expected to make a pilgrimage or *hajj* to Mecca, once during his life. Upon arrival at Mecca, he goes round the Ka 'aba seven times, then kisses the holy Black Stone. After making the pilgrimage a Muslim may call himself Hajji and wear a green band round his head.

Mosques

The Muslim place of worship is called a mosque. These are usually very beautiful buildings with domes and minarets. Mohammed disapproved of making pictures or statues of human beings or of God. Because of this, mosques are decorated with abstract or geometric designs, or particularly beautiful Arabic writing of phrases from the Qur'an.

Muezzins call fellow Muslims to prayer from the top of a minaret. Shoes are removed before entering the mosque. There are no seats inside, for the floor is covered with prayer carpets at prayer time. When praying, a Muslim kneels and bows his head to the ground. All the congregation face Mecca. The *Imam*, or leader, reads and explains verses from the Qur'an and urges worshippers to live a good life.

Strict laws

Like Jews, Muslims have very strict laws about the food they eat. They are also forbidden to drink alcohol or to gamble.

Muslim women are expected to wear clothes that completely cover their bodies. Although modern fashions are now reaching Muslim countries, many women continue to wear a veil over their heads and the loose trousers that cover their legs.

On the whole, Muslim women stay at home. They do not often visit the mosque, but worship Allah in the peace of their own homes.

Islam today

Even when they live in non Islamic countries, Muslims try to follow Allah's teachings. Even when working in a modern factory, a good Muslim will unfold his prayer mat and, turning towards Mecca, he will pray, as instructed in the Qur'an. There are many thousands of Muslims now living in England. They have built mosques and they remain faithful to the Five Pillars of Wisdom, even when this is difficult.

A Muslim says his prayers in Jerusalem. In the background is the famous Dome of the Rock, a mosque built by Omar on the site of Abraham's attempted sacrifice of his son, Isaac.

Religious development

In addition to the older religions described in this book, a number of different religious groups have emerged during the past hundred years. Usually this has happened because people have been unable to find what they were looking for in the established religions.

Mormons

Among new religions, the Mormons or Latter Day Saints are probably the oldest. Joseph Smith, the founder, believed he had seen God, Jesus Christ and the Angel Moroni. The Angel showed him some golden plates on which was written an account of how some of God's people, the Jews, had come to America in the 6th century BC and their descendants were visited by Jesus Christ.

After his death, a group of Mormons led by Brigham Young, travelled one thousand miles to the Great Salt Lake in the state of Utah.

▲ Rastafarians believe that they are the true people of God. Many look forward to the day when they can return to Ethiopia, the black man's home. This religion began in Jamaica. It contains elements of Judaism and Christianity. They believe in black power, pacifism and the dignity of black people.

The Salvation Army was started in 1861 by William Booth to help the poor and the needy. It is now a world movement. ▼

Mormons continue to believe that God talks to them directly. Their young men spend two years travelling about spreading their ideas.

They give up ten per cent of their surplus income to the church and they are forbidden to drink alcohol, tea or coffee.

Jehovah's Witnesses

Founded by Charles Taze Russell in 1881 in the USA, the Witnesses take their name from the Bible: 'Ye are my witnesses saith the Lord, that I am God.' Their belief is based completely on the words of the Bible.

Christian Science

Mary Baker Eddy founded Christian Science in Boston, USA. She believed that her faith in God and Christ had cured her of a serious injury. Her book states that since God is good and created man in his own image, then sickness, sadness and sin cannot be associated with him. By faith and prayer, people can be rid of these things.

▲ The Hare Krishna sect follow the teachings of Rama Krishna. They believe in love and peace and wear yellow robes and shave their heads. Eastern religions have begun to influence people in the West and now have many followers.

Some religions have been much influenced by others. This Fetish shrine in Ghana has statues of local gods and of the Bible's Adam and Eve. ▼

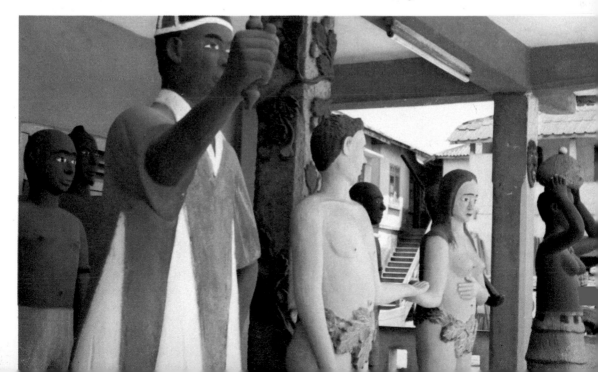

Two philosophies

During the past few hundred years, a growing number of people in the West have not felt the need to believe in the existence of God. They think men should find happiness and a good life by themselves without divine help.

In the twentieth century, this is easier than it has ever been, since more people enjoy a higher standard of living. Religious belief is declining in the West as people are more interested in getting material possessions.

Life was very different in previous centuries when the great majority of people lived poverty-stricken, hard working lives and few could hope to better themselves. Before the Reformation, the Christian Church taught men to be content with their life on earth and to look forward to a better life with God, after death.

Humanism

Early Humanists were not atheists, that is people who do not believe in God, but they did believe in the right of every human to make the best of their lives. Humanists wanted to make the world a better place, not for the love of God or in the hope of life after death, but because they thought it was right. They believed in truth, tolerance and concern for other people.

Modern Humanists

They believe that every man has the right to freedom of thought, speech and employment. They consider that religion is no longer necessary in a scientific age.

▲ Karl Marx, a German who lived in England, was the founder of Communism. He believed that people should own all the land and they should work not for profit but for the good of everyone.

Materialism

Materialism is a doctrine that there is neither a supernatural or spiritual world. All that exists is the physical world in which we live. Russia and China, two of the largest and most powerful countries in the world follow the ideas of Communism, a political philosophy based on the doctrine of materialism. Communist theory states that man can control this material, or physical world. The idea of an all powerful spiritual being is not accepted. Religious belief is discouraged. Communism draws conclusions about the way society should be organized by studying the way it has developed in the past. One claim is that non-Communist societies must eventually collapse.

△ Some Chinese people carry a picture of their famous Communist leader, Mao Tse Tung. Lenin, Trotsky and Stalin were important Russian Communists.

Sheffield in 1884. The terrible condition of the workers in factories and slums like this horrified Marx and inspired him to write his book, *Das Kapital*.▼

Star of David

wheel: Hindu, Buddhist

statue of Buddha

Om: Hindu

Celtic cross

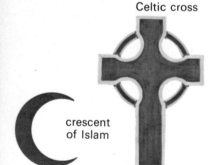

crescent of Islam

▲ Symbols of the major religions. Om, a sacred Hindu word, represents their three main gods. The Celtic cross is one of the many Christian crosses.
The Buddhist temple at Bodnath, Nepal. The eyes stand for the all-seeing eyes of the Buddha. ▶

Some common qualities

If you look at several religions you will notice some similarities between them. You could make a list of these similarities. To help you begin here are some of them.

Brotherhood and prayer

Nearly all religions expect believers to help others. This has led to the spread of education, medical care and help for the helpless.

Most believers are expected to pray regularly, praising and thanking God and asking for his help. Some men and women give up the pleasures of the world and spend their entire lives in prayer and meditation.

Most religions possess a sacred or holy book. This contains the commandments of their God and the sayings of their prophets and holy men.

Places of worship

All religions have special places which people can visit for worship individually at any time or together at special times.

The city of Jerusalem is important to three religions: Islam, Judaism and Christianity. It contains the Mosque of Omar, often called the Dome of the Rock, The Wailing Wall and many churches at sites associated with Christ.

Celebrations and festivals

Most religions celebrate important events in the history of their religion or in the life of the founder. They offer exciting and happy interruptions to everyday life. Festivals which celebrate the life of Christ have sometimes taken over the dates of ancient pagan feasts.

Personal happiness

Religions have taught a system of behaviour by which men of that faith can live in peace with each other. This has done much to make life easier and happier for mankind. Some religions also teach hope and faith in a life after death. This has brought comfort to millions and made difficult lives easier to bear.

Index

Illustrations appear in bold type.

Abraham 24, **24**, 35, 37
Adi Granth 22
Ahura Mazda 23
Amritsar **22**

Baptism 30, **31, 33**
Baptist 33
Bar Mitzvah 26, **26**
Benares **17**
Booth, William 38
Brahma 14, **14,** 15
Brahman 14, **14,** 15, 16
Buddha 18, 19, **19, 42**
Buddhism 18, 20
Byzantine 34

Calvin, John 32
Caste system **14,** 15
Christian 30, 31, 40, 42
Christian Science 39
Christianity 28, 29, 34, 35
Church of England 33
Communism 40
Confirmation 30
Confucianism 20
Crucifixion 29, **29, 30,** 31

Divali 15, 16
Dome of the Rock **37,** 42

Eddy, Mary Baker 39
Eightfold Path 18, 19, 20
Egypt 8, 9, 24, 25, 27

Five K's 22
Five Pillars of Wisdom 35, 37
Four Noble Truths 19
Funeral 31

Ganges **17**
Garden of Eden 35
Gautama, Prince Siddhartha 18
Goliath **25**
Good Friday 31

Hades 11
Hajji 36
Hare Krishna **39**
Harijan 15
Hassidic Jews **27**
Hebrew 24
Hijra 34
Hindu 14, 15, 16, **17,** 18, 22, 23, 42

Holi 16
Holy Communion 30
Holy Eastern Orthodox Church 29, 30
Holy Land 13
Humanism 40

Id-Al-Fitr 36
Iman 37
Incense 9, 11
India 14, 15
Isaac **24,** 37
Islam 22, 34, 35, 37
Israel 13

Jains 22, **22,** 23
Japan 20
Jehovah's Witnesses 39
Jerusalem 26, **37,** 42
Jesus Christ 28, 29, **29,** 30, 31, 35, 38, 42
Jews 13, 24, 25, 27, 28, 38
Judaism 24, 28, 34, 35, 38

Ka'aba 34, 36, **36**
Kamidanu 21
Kosher 26
Krishna 14, **15,** 16
Kshatrya **14,** 15

Lenin 41
Luther 42

Mahayana Buddhism 20
Marx, Karl **40,** 41
Mass 30
Materialism 40
Mecca 34, 36, 37
Medina 34
Messiah 30
Methodism 33
Missionary 12, 13
Mohammed 34, 35, 36
Monastery 18
Monks 19
Mormons 38, 39
Moses 24, 25
Mosque 36, 37, **37**
Mount Olympus 10
Muezzin 37
Mummy 9, **9**
Muslim 34, 35, 36, 37

Nam 22
Neptune 11
New Testament 30
Nirvana 19
Nonconformist 32, 33

Palestine 24, 25
Papyrus 8
Pariahs **14,** 15

Parsee 23, **23**
Passover 27, 30
Penn, William **32,** 33
Pilgrim Fathers 32
Pilgrimage 36
Presbyterian 32
Protestant 29, 32
Puritans 32, **32**

Quakers 32, **32,** 33
Qur'an 35, 36, 37

Ramadan 35, 36
Re 8
Reformation 32, 40
Reincarnation 23
Resurrection 29
Roman Catholicism 29, 32
Roman Empire 9, 11, 28, 29

Sangha 19
Scroll 8, 25, **25**
Shabbat 26
Shinto 20, 21
Shiva 14
Shofar **24,** 25, 27
Shrine 9, 20, 21, **21**
Sikh 22, **22, 23**
Smith, Joseph 38
Stalin 41
Star of David **42**
Styx **11**
Sudras **14,** 15
Sumeria 24

Talmud 25
Taoism 20, **20**
Temple 9, 10, 11, 15, **20,** 22, **22,** 23, **23, 43**
Ten Commandments 25
Torah 25, 26
Tori 21, **21**
Totem pole **6**
Towers of Silence 23
Tung, Mao Tse **41**
Tutankhamun **9**

Untouchables **14,** 15
Ur 24

Vaisyas **14,** 15
Vishnu 14, **15**

Wailing Wall **27,** 42
Wedding 16, **17,** 31
Wesley, John 33, **33**

Yom Kippur 27
Young, Brigham 38

Zen 10, 11
Zoroastra 23